Wiltshire Industrial History

Working class episodes

The Swing Rebellion

Chartism in Wiltshire

Trowbridge communist councillors

The Trowbridge Martyr

Socialism in Swindon

WaterMarx

Published by WaterMarx on behalf of
White Horse (Wiltshire) Trades Council.
Based on a series of talks given at a local history day-school at St
Margaret's Hall, Bradford on Avon on 6 November 2010

Published in 2011
by
WaterMarx
www.watermarx.co.uk
on behalf of
White Horse (Wiltshire) Trades Council

ISBN 978-0-9570726-0-2

Printed by Sarum Colourview
Unit 8, Woodford Centre
Lysander Way, Old Sarum, Salisbury SP4 6BU
01722 343 600
www.sarumcolourview.co.uk

Contents

Cover picture by Clifford Harper©

Introduction

by Rosie MacGregor
Chair, White Horse (Wiltshire) Trades Union Council

It has been the case throughout history that the stories of the common man and woman are rarely recorded with the same vigour as the exploits of the wealthy and powerful.

Hardly surprising in an unequal society where pen and paper, as well as the ability to read or write, were normally the prerogative of those with money and an education.

Where detailed records were kept, the stories were often one sided, exaggerating the claims of those that held power. Reliance on word of mouth rather than the written page had been the fate of the poor, whose views often ran counter to the opinions of their wealthy masters.

Such has been the case in Wiltshire where, even today, few outside Trowbridge know the tragic story of Thomas Helliker; where only a minority in the county are aware of the extent of the Swing Rebellion; or that Chartism played a significant role in the lives of the ordinary people.

The oppression suffered by the working classes together with stories of their misfortune and fights for justice have been largely forgotten. As have the names of local working class heroes like Phyllis and Idris Rose, Communist Councillors in Trowbridge in the 1960s, or the story of Derique Montaut, Trades Union activist

Rosie MacGregor chairing the history day in St Margaret's Hall, Bradford on Avon

Picture by Bob Naylor©

and subsequent leader of the Labour Group on Swindon Council, during which time the Labour vote doubled.

It was for this reason the White Horse (Wiltshire) Trades Union Council decided to hold a local history day in the autumn of 2010 under the banner of Wiltshire History Day, Working Class Episodes. The predecessor of the current trades council, Trowbridge TUC, known latterly as West Wiltshire TUC, had in the past organised a number of successful lectures to commemorate the life of Thomas Helliker, but little record remains of these.

Trades Councils, organised through the TUC, have a huge role in campaigning and raising awareness of what is happening in the trades union movement and in the community. It was felt, in this instance, that there was a gap in the collective memory about working class history in Wiltshire that needed to be addressed.

Once the decision to hold the event had been taken, the content considered, and different speakers, all experts in their own field invited, things moved forward very quickly.

The venue St Margaret's Hall in Bradford on Avon was selected because not only was it relatively central to the area covered by the local trades council, from Malmesbury in the north to Westbury and Warminster in the south, but it was easily accessible by public transport.

The organisers were delighted with the attendance. One member of the audience had even travelled from as far away as Barnstable in North Devon. It was generally agreed it had been a huge success with memorable and informative talks from each of the speakers. There were sincere, moving and inspirational stories, as well as occasional humour to be drawn from the foibles and weakness of humankind.

It is hoped that this book will be a testament to the many different stories and cultural roots of the working people of Wiltshire.

White Horse (Wiltshire) Trades Council is grateful to Newsquest Wiltshire, publishers of the Wiltshire Times, Wiltshire Gazette & Herald and the Swindon Advertiser for permission to use their press cuttings and to Devizes Town Council for permission to use the poster at the bottom of page 17.

Trowbridge Communist Councillors

Phyllis and Idris Rose

by Dave Chapple

The election of communist councillors in any town or city in England in the second half of the 20th Century was an unusual event. When this happened, it was not in the places a socialist might expect. In the West Country, communists were elected in Clevedon, Cirencester, Bradford on Avon and Trowbridge.

In Clevedon, my home town, there was a communist councillor for 20-odd years, usually elected unopposed. Bert Searle was one of the most popular men in town, starting from pre-war days when, as a baker, he gave free bread to the unemployed. The 'folk' memory of that generosity held him in good stead for the next 40 years.

Wogan Phillips, 2nd Baron of Milford, was, believe it or not, a Communist Party councillor in Cirencester, and a member of the House of Lords for a short while in the late 1940s!

HS Turner, a research chemist, was elected for Bradford on Avon Urban District Council in 1946 from no less than 31 candidates, at 4.45am, in front of a crowd of 200 people!

Idris Rose was born in 1906 and died aged 70 on 20th February 1976. He had been a communist councillor on Trowbridge UDC for the twelve years between May 1961 and 1973. He was joined in 1969 by his wife Phyllis, who then became part of what was, perhaps, the only husband and wife team of communist urban district councillors in British history.

So why did this happen in Trowbridge? And was this socially and politically significant as well as unusual?

From 1946, Idris Rose worked and campaigned for fifteen years to get elected to the council. He had been an active Trowbridge communist before the Second World War. In his inadequate and patronizing tribute to Idris when he died in 1976, Wiltshire Times columnist 'The Gleaner' recalled first coming across Idris Rose in the summer of 1939, selling copies of the Daily Worker on "a miserable Saturday afternoon in the gutter" outside the gas showrooms in Court Street:

"Trowbridge will miss its Communist... though you might detest and oppose the political party that inspired the public activities of Idris Rose... you could not help but admire the indomitable persistence in putting forward what he believed in. There was something both splendid and oddly pathetic about him..."

To answer the question "Why Trowbridge?" it is necessary to understand a little of what this town and west Wiltshire were like in the 1950s and 1960s, how the Urban District Council functioned, the activities of the local Communist Party and, finally, to recognize the unusual drive and energy of Idris Rose as a socialist and trades unionist.

Trowbridge and west Wiltshire in the early 1960s

So what sort of place was west Wiltshire? Well, the Chairman of the Trowbridge UDC in 1961, Councillor J Ladd, called it a time of "competition, profits and prosperity."

Let's look at the Wiltshire Times. In 1961 the town's main employers were Bowyers (sausages), Ushers brewery; Sainsburys, Palmers, Clarks, Wiltshire United Dairies, Nestles, McCalls, Newman Henders, Waldens, Sandys and Knees. Many of these factories were expanding.

There was an immigrant West Indian population in west Wiltshire, mainly working-class factory workers. This subject deserves to be thoroughly researched while oral testimony is still available.

The Trowbridge woollen industry, which once inspired the moniker 'Manchester of the West', had survived. The Wiltshire Times reported a retirement presentation to Bert Vince of Studley Mill Cottage, Trowbridge. He had worked for 53 years at Clarks Mill, starting work at Stallard Street when he was 13, for 8 shillings a week. One of his boyhood jobs had been lighting the gas lamps over the looms. He also worked on what was known as the bumble picker, used for stirring and shaking up wool. Then he went into the dye house and then the boiler house where he was a stoker for about 30 years. All his life he had lived in a house that was owned by the mill.

During the 1950s and 1960s right-wing councils accepted what a later Tory Government rejected: that the building of new council housing was a civic duty. Local housing for key workers was being planned by the "small 'c' " conservatives who controlled the Trowbridge UDC. They were also building a whole new council estate of 4-500 houses between Upper Studley and Bradley Rd, to add to those at Longfield and Seymour. In 1962 there were 165 houses in Trowbridge condemned as slums, 90 of which would be demolished in the next four years. By 1962 Trowbridge had new bus and fire stations, and the town's Further Education College was in full use.

There was a protest letter in the Wiltshire Times about the cost of fish and chips, complaining that 5oz of chips cost 8d, which equated to over 2 shillings per lb, when potatoes in the shops were being sold for only 3d per lb!

The Post Office had just introduced Subscriber Trunk Dialling (STD) in Chippenham.

The Agricultural Labourer's Union, the NUAW, still had 130 village branches in Somerset in the 1960s and I am sure Wiltshire was no different. In February 1962 there was a presentation of £750 from JC Coe, NUAW County Organiser, to WJ Hinks of Sutton Parva, an agricultural worker who was medically retired after an accident.

A 15-year-old girl was sent to a remand home for three months for assessment. She had stolen a powder compact and tube of eye shadow from another girl's purse at a rock and roll dance at Trowbridge Town Hall's Top 20 Club. She collapsed in court shouting that she would rather die than go to that remand home.

On 21st April 1961 the same Top 20 Club had Johnny Carr and the Cadillacs, backed by Johnny Mile and the Shades, at a cost of 3 shillings entrance. Local crooner Danny Davies was also playing the Top 20 Club, with Shirley Day and the Semitones. Meanwhile, Melksham Assembly Hall had Ken Eaten and his Orchestra, which sounds as though the audience would be an older generation, but, by popular request, he played some Rock and Roll during his session. The Laverton Institute in Westbury had a Teen and 20 Club where you could see Dean Prime and the Dukes for 3 shillings.

The Trowbridge British Legion Bugle Band was in trouble but would soldier on.

There were at least half a dozen cinemas in west Wiltshire. The Gaumont in Trowbridge had 'Pure Hell of St Trinians', The Maxine at Melksham had 'Hannibal', with Victor Mature, backed up by Bugs Bunny Cartoon No1, while the Vista at Westbury had 'Let No Man Write my Epitaph' with Burl Ives and Shelley Winters.

Trowbridge Town FC entered the Southern League around this time. Their home gates were 7-800, well down from the 2,500 who regularly watched Western League games in 1958/9, let alone their record gate of 9,009 for an FA Cup qualifying round tie with Weymouth in 1949, but substantial support nonetheless.

The Wiltshire Working Men's Conservative Benefit Society had its 74th Annual General Meeting at Holloway House Trowbridge and the Grand Master, a retired Brigadier, EL Luce, reported a small but steady decline in membership over the previous 10 years or so.

The national Bow Group of Conservative MPs had proposed that Trowbridge be transformed into a city of 300,000 people! Meanwhile, local Tories boasted that the town had more car parks than any other town in the West of England.

Legendary Wiltshire peace campaigner Austin Underwood inspired 600 cars to attend the Imber lost village trespass campaign on 22nd January 1961.

There was a strong Co-operative Society in which Phyllis and Idris were involved. In the Wiltshire Times of May 26th 1961, when the Co-op announced that it had gained 428 new members in six months, Phyllis Rose said this:

'COUNCILLORS WORSHIP AT SHRINE OF PROFIT'
Trowbridge allotment sale attack by Mr. Rose

THE WILTSHIRE TIMES, FRIDAY, JULY 20, 1962
Mr. Rose Objects To New U.D.C. Standing Orders

"Perhaps you feel that we are always attacking the Co-op, but we are out to build it!"

The population of Trowbridge in 1961 was around 16,000: the Trowbridge and District Co-op Society had 15,700 members! They had a village branch at Holt that even had its own Co-operative Society Library run by Mrs L Alford.

The Labour Party in west Wiltshire

Jack Hayes, Gordon Brewer, Wilfred Aslett, Hugh Arkwright and Mr & Mrs Male were the stalwarts of the Trowbridge Labour Party. Right-winger Jack Hayes, one of the Roses' key opponents, was first elected to the UDC in 1953, had been a poll-topper three years running and

was Chairman of the UDC in 1962. When he lost heavily in 1968, Hayes' bitterness that his moderation was not appreciated by the Tories was revealed:

"I am disappointed. I always concentrated on impartiality."

In nearby Melksham, FB Day was a County Councillor and Cllr Mary Salisbury had been the Labour standard-bearer for decades. Corsham Labour Party had Central Ammunition Depot ganger WD Pope.

Westbury, where Labour had already run the UDC and Phyllis Cundick was the County Councillor, was still very much the working-class railway town it had been for 80 years. March 1961, for example, saw a retirement presentation by AE Griffiths, ASLEF General Secretary, to Westbury train driver Tom Parker. Tom had worked 50 years on the railway and had been a Westbury UDC Labour councillor for no less than 24 years, beginning in 1937.

But 1961 was not a good year for west Wiltshire socialists. Labour County Councillors such as Molly Mixen in Bradford and Hugh Arkwright, a left-winger in Trowbridge North, lost their seats.

There is ample evidence from the Wiltshire Times of the common discrepancy between the radicalism of the well-supported local Labour Parties, and the conservatism of Labour councillors.

In March 1961, for example, 53 delegates at the AGM of the Westbury Constituency Labour Party voted for motions asking that 1% of GDP goes to 'underprivileged people'; and that the Socialist Medical Association is supported to oppose NHS charges, on the grounds that charges '…depart from the principle of a Health Service free at the point of need.'

Two months later, 36 delegates at the Trowbridge Trades and Labour Club voted to adopt a Bechuanaland transit refugee camp, and to make a donation to the Nye Bevan Memorial Fund. April 1961 saw the membership of the Bradford and Trowbridge Young Socialists increase by 20%.

Understanding how Idris and Phyllis Rose, with politics in most respects to the left of Labour, came to represent Trowbridge workers on the council, might start at this point in the story. I hope I have established that there was, by English standards, in west Wiltshire in the early 1960s, quite an advanced working class social and political culture. But what were the obstacles?

Peter Allison was the Labour Agent for the Westbury Constituency Labour Party, which included Trowbridge. His reaction to the 1961 County Council setbacks was to state, "The public were duped by the smoke-screen of Independence."

This was true. The dominant Trowbridge political tradition right up to the 1960s was of 'Independents' or 'Ratepayers'. These councillors were nearly all reactionaries — conservatives with a big or a small 'c'. In contrast, the Labour opposition in these towns usually declared its colours.

It was this reactionary Trowbridge UDC, including some very cautious Labour members, which for twelve years struggled to cope with the election of Phyllis and Idris Rose.

In those years, it was extremely difficult for Labour or Communist supporters to become councilors, because employers were still showing a reluctance to release working class Labour candidates from work.

Many Labour councillors, some of them victimized pre-war trades unionists, became Co-op collectors and insurance agents for benefit societies, to get around this problem. Another way was to rely on working-class patronage to become self-employed: Idris Rose himself was a

self-employed painter and decorator for thirty years.

Trowbridge elects a Communist!

When Idris was elected in May 1961, deposing Labour's Gordon Brewer, he got stuck in right away and, within a year, he had climbed from ninth and last-elected councilor, to second from top of the poll in 1962, when an impressive 1808 Trowbridge people voted for him. On that election night he was reported as saying, "The poll is fantastic. It has surpassed all expectations: we had the whole of the Labour machine against us; we were in fact fighting both factions".

Idris said that he was extremely proud to think that Trowbridge people had cast everything aside and voted so readily for him.

"They are clear sighted enough to see what work a councillor of my type can do. I now ask everyone who voted for me to support me outside the Council Chamber as well as inside because you should understand that you as well as myself have to play this vital role in determining the policy of Trowbridge Town Council."

Mr Rose was carried shoulder high from the Town Hall to a chorus of 'For He's a Jolly Good Fellow'. The sensational election of a Trowbridge Communist inspired Independent Councillor JED Brindley to Churchillian heights of rhetoric: "In the humdrum existence of a peaceful and prosperous country town like Trowbridge, few are put to the test of proving themselves worthy and loyal members of a community so typical of Old England, but the recent Council election makes one wonder how far from the heritage which was traditional of an English people can present-day electors wander?"

Chairman of the Council, the Independent J Ladd added this: "For the past year this Council has watched the way Mr Rose has conducted himself in his work on the Council, sometimes with dismay and often with disgust. From now on, so far as I am concerned, the gloves are off and I am going to tell Mr Rose why in the committees' opinion he was not placed on these two committees."

The ruling Independent councillors prevented Idris from being on the Housing Committee because they said he knew the council tenants too well! He was also prevented from sitting on the Finance and General Purposes Committee.

Trowbridge Labour and Communist Parties

Peter Allison's reaction in 1961 had shared some of the Independent's near-hysteria: "We are sorry that a vast number of electors in Trowbridge voted for the Communist candidate... their aim is to stand more candidates until they get control of the council."

In 1962, faced with a massive increase in the communist vote, Peter Allison, in a more subtle criticism of working-class voters, complained that many of them voted ONLY for the communist candidate.

"Because of apathy on the part of electorate we now have our first Communist Councilor. They will not rest until they have two Communist councilors."

Acrimonious public discussions with Peter Allison followed. Idris Rose suggested an electoral pact so that Phyllis would not stand against a Labour councillor. Between 1961 and her eventual success in 1969, she was getting closer every year to being elected. But Peter Allison turned the offer of a pact down flat.

Jack Hayes, the veteran Labour councillor in Trowbridge, manipulated council agendas so that, after 1963, Idris was prevented from moving motions in council because they had to be seconded before going on the agenda. It was only when Phyllis was finally elected in 1969 that this changed.

This implies that out of the four or five reasonably progressive Labour councillors, none

was willing to risk condemnation by their own party to second Idris Rose's attempts to bring politics and world affairs into Trowbridge Urban District Council Chamber. Notwithstanding justifiable Labour anger at splitting the working-class vote, I think that says a lot about the Trowbridge Labour Party at the time.

Idris Rose and the Trowbridge communists — 18-strong in 1963 — held regular public meetings, sometimes in the streets, right into the 1970s. As late as 1973, during his unsuccessful campaign to get elected to the new West Wiltshire District Council, Idris held two factory gate meetings at Bowyers and Newman Henders. He also held two Market Day meetings, many street meetings and loudspeaker tours, and delivered 7,000 communist leaflets.

He always believed strongly that if socialists were elected onto the council, and took it over, then it could become a formidable Wiltshire campaigning body against Tory Government policy.

Stamping as 'Communist' Councillor Calls for Ban on Bomb

BRISTOL EVENING WORLD, WEDNESDAY, JANUARY 24, 1962

Council Housing and World Peace

For many years prior to Idris' election in 1961 he was a leading organiser of the Trowbridge Council Tenants Association, which became a major base for his increasing electoral popularity. Not surprisingly, once he became a councillor, improving Trowbridge housing was his number one priority. This meant demolishing the remaining slums, improving the council housing stock and building new council houses at affordable rents.

Trowbridge communists also called for the repeal of the Revaluation Act, and for the government to bring down interest charges of housing to 2%, to restore the housing subsidy to its 1946 value. One issue of the Trowbridge Leader, the Trowbridge CPGB Branch newsletter, made the political point that Urban District Councils and Boroughs were charged extortionate interest rates to borrow to build houses in the first place, which then was clawed back from the tenants through rent rises.

Locally, communist policy was to have no rent increases, to restore the local rates subsidy and pay only the statutory amount of £8 a year per house, instead of the proposed £15 into the repairs account, and also to balance the housing revenue account with the surplus in the housing repairs account.

Idris Rose was strongly opposed to Trowbridge Urban District Council and local rate payers subsidising some very profitable large national firms, who could well afford to build or provide houses for their own workers. He argued that there should not be a single house allocated to a key worker at firms such as Bowyers, Ushers, Nestles and United Dairies, while local lower-paid workers languished on the waiting list.

In a typical 1960s election campaign, Idris, Phyllis and the Trowbridge Communist Party delivered between 7,000 and 10,000 leaflets and copies of the Trowbridge Leader. Most issues concentrated on housing and rent rises. In 1963, the "Trowbridge Leader", during the Christine Keeler affair, reported that Idris and the Trowbridge Communist Party were demanding an immediate General Election.

Idris Rose did not confine his energies to housing. He caused another kerfuffle in the local newspaper by raising the issue of nuclear weapons. Before 1960 the Communist Party had opposed unilateralism at the behest of the Kremlin, but in 1960, when the famous Labour Party Conference debate took place, the Labour Party became unilateralist and the Communist Party followed suit.

Idris reported in council that Amesbury Rural District Council was concerned about possible radiation of the atmosphere on the farm crops and food chain. On February 9th 1962 he moved a council motion calling for the banning and an end to the testing of nuclear weapons. In his right of reply he contemptuously dismissed the opposition as "typical of bourgeois thought... there is this class struggle... all this money for war, yet no money for improvements to Back St, Stallard St, no new hospital, still our obsolete Parochial School."

This was exemplary socialist councillorship.

Idris Rose had visited Romania as a delegate from the Communist Party West of England District in 1957. His attitude to Joe Stalin and the East German-Hungarian revolts is not known. He was almost certainly no dissident communist. He believed that the Soviet Union was a socialist state. He believed in world peace passionately, and raised this in the Town Hall council chamber as well as the Wiltshire Times, but he recognized, as did CPGB policy, that world peace meant peaceful co-existence with a stable capitalist west. Idris also raised the issue of British Empire liberation struggles in Malaya, Cyprus and Aden.

Passionate public politics did not go down well at all with all his fellow councillors. Independent councillor JC McDonald spluttered out to the press, "In my 18 years on Council I have never ever heard politics before. Why is Mr Rose doing this to the town?"

Idris Rose championed allotment holders and on one occasion 50 allotment holders crowded the council chamber whilst he advocated their rights.

Idris and Phyllis lived at 119 Newtown, next to the Trowbridge Trades and Labour Club. An ideal residence for communist public figures, but inconvenient when disgruntled or inebriated men and women knocked on the Roses' door, demanding something or other at half past ten at night!

In 1964, the Communist Party magazine Country Standard reported that Idris was no mean skittles player, which must have brought this Marxist educated man into contact with a hell of a lot of men and women who practiced this West Country quasi-religious rite.

Idris Rose was a member of CND and, together with Labour Party CND activist Hugh Arkwright, organised walkers' training sessions for the April 1962 Aldermaston March. For five weeks they met at 2.30 every Sunday afternoon by the Park Club and completed a 10-mile walk.

Unfortunately, I have found out little about Phyllis Rose. From 1960 onwards, when Idris was about to go on the council she had attended every council meeting to take notes and write letters to the Wiltshire Times. Although this might have appeared to be merely a supportive role for her husband, Phyllis was actually working towards being elected herself. Idris and Phyllis had a daughter, Gloria Harvey. Hopefully we can find out more about Phyllis.

The council careers of Idris and Phyllis Rose came to an end with the abolition of Trowbridge UDC in April 1974. In 2011 that fine old Town Hall, scene of rock and roll hops as well as those passionate arguments between the advocates of capitalism and communism, stands empty and forlorn.

One of the tragedies of English 20th century political history was the Labour Party's support, in government and in opposition, for the abolition of Borough Councils and UDCs. Many of these, even in the West Country, were Labour controlled and some — Bridgwater Borough Council, for instance — were very progressive indeed. At a stroke, they were wiped out on 1st April 1974. Idris did stand for the new West Wiltshire District Council in 1973, but came thirteenth in an election for nine places. He had three years left to live, and, thwarted politically, spent these to the full, as an active Trowbridge trades unionist.

Trowbridge Trades Union Council

Idris Rose had always been a trades unionist. In the early 1960s, like all CPGB trades union members, he had been the victim of the TUC's Black Circular which banned communists from becoming trades council delegates. When this ban was lifted, Idris lost little time getting involved. Branch Secretary of the National Federation of Building Trade Operatives, an important confederation of trades unions, he was a delegate to Trowbridge and District Trades Council, from NFBTO, and later UCATT, during the late 1960s and early 1970s. This was a relatively halcyon time for trades unions, when Wiltshire boasted Trades Councils in Melksham, Warminster, Chippenham, Salisbury, Swindon, Devizes and Trowbridge.

These trades council meetings were well-attended — twenty delegates was not unusual — well-reported, and they had some local clout. At various times, Idris was Chair and Vice-Chair of the Trades Council and there he brought his

socialist beliefs before his fellow trades unionists.

Trowbridge Trades Council was concerned about Ireland. In 1972 Idris Rose arranged speakers from both the Connolly Association, the famous author and intellectual Desmond Greaves, but also the Troops Out Movement, which was certainly not controlled by the Communist Party.

Trowbridge Trades Council fought the Tories' Industrial Relations Act in the early 1970s. Some unions had registered with the Act, unlike the building workers who, with the NUM, TGWU and other unions, led the battle against the Ted Heath government.

One fascinating piece in the Trades Council's minutes describes a group of five women from the Trowbridge Women's Movement, led by Dianne Brown, who demanded that five women should attend the next meeting to put the demands of the Working Women's Charter... one of which, no doubt, was to make the trades union movement less male and more radical!

Last and definitely not least of Idris Rose's trades union activities was his support for The Shrewsbury Pickets, arrested during the 1972 building workers' strike. In 2011 there is a renewed campaign for amnesty and pardon for the surviving Shrewsbury Pickets, including the truly heroic Des Warren who died in jail, at the hands of the state. On 15th June 1974, with Idris Rose as Chair, the Trades Council passed this motion: "While welcoming the release on bail of Bros Des Warren and Ricky Tomlinson, we nevertheless realize the danger of the 1875 Criminal Trespass Law, and call for its repeal, together with the quashing of the convictions of the Shrewsbury Pickets."

There exists a disturbing correspondence in the Wiltshire and Swindon History Centre between Trowbridge TUC and Alex Lyon, Labour Home Secretary, which reveals that the Labour Government of the mid-late 1970s was deliberately doing nothing to get the pickets out of jail.

Other trades council motions in the early 1970s included demanding an inquiry into police actions at the Red Lion Square demonstration and opposition to council house evictions and distraint of furniture. The wording of this was memorable: "...in this scientific age of 1975 we should not tolerate the horrible and shameful ways of the 1930s. It is a fault of the capitalist system: in the Soviet Union rents have not risen for decades. We regard housing as a social service."

During 1975, trades council meetings at the Ship Inn, Frome Road were attended by an average of only ten delegates out of a total of twenty-five, with ten branches affiliated. The decline of the trades council's movement, only recently halted, was gathering pace.

Conclusion

In the great majority of elections contested by Phyllis and Idris they were opposed by Labour Party candidates. This made their election to office all the more positive — a verdict of the Trowbridge working class and its determination to criticize and consciously go beyond the limitations of a stale 'Labourism.'

Communist Party strategy in the 1960s and 1970s, embodied in 'The British Road to Socialism', was to elect a Labour government with the maximum number of Communist Party MPs, to keep that government on the parliamentary road to socialism. Trowbridge revealed a fault in this strategy because if Trowbridge workers could 'see through' Labour, why not the whole of the working-class? Why not the CPGB itself? Was, in fact, the CPGB's Labour Government strategy honest? Surely they knew that Labour was incapable of ever delivering a socialist government?

I think this story of Trowbridge communism is of more than merely historical interest. It is not just an anomaly, a curiosity. What we had in Trowbridge for twelve years were 2000 Trowbridge working class people who thought that the Labour Party was not progressive enough, that the Labour Party was not socialist enough, even anti-socialist, and who were prepared to go out and vote for an alternative.

In Trowbridge the gloves were off. The Labour Party, independents and communists were fighting for seats, and the communists came out on top.

But why Trowbridge? Is it in cities, towns or villages that people got angriest against the established order? We should not assume change always begins in cities. Some of the most hard-line, angry, militant communities in 20th Century British history were the mining villages of the Rhondda, Chopwell in Durham and Lumphinnans in Fife.

West Wiltshire towns and villages at one point in its history had surpassed those 'Little Moscows' for militancy: — the revolutionary Chartist days of the 1830s and 1840s. The huge Staverton Mill was burnt to the ground; seven thousand assembled on Trowle Common; pikes were being sharpened at village blacksmiths; pistols and muskets were being ordered from Bath; and a Blue Plaque please for the Trowbridge pharmacist who was given a three-year jail sentence in 1839 for putting bullets in his window marked 'pills for the Tories'!

Trowbridge and west Wiltshire was, in contrast, not a militant area in the 1960s. But its working class culture was confident, stable and highly developed. This culture included a council tenants' association; trades union branches and workplace shop stewards; a successful and popular Co-operative Society; Labour and Communist Party Branches; allotment associations; working class sports leagues for darts, crib and skittles — and a good semi-professional soccer team.

Trowbridge was a town of a size — less than 20,000 — where most of the active members of all these groups would know each other: this may be key. It is doubtful if that local working-class grapevine could be as effective in much larger towns or cities split into districts. If this guess is accurate, then Idris and Phyllis lived in the best town at the best time to do the job they did.

If revolution in Trowbridge in 1961/2 was long-gone as a Communist Party aim, Idris and Phyllis Rose brought some very important local, national and international questions of a socialist nature to the Trowbridge Town Hall. In doing so, they overturned the sedate conservative traditions of an Urban District Council, with its points of order and its chairman's badge of office and its procedural prevarications. They incited Tory outrage and instigated a communal debate on vital matters.

Did it have to be the Communist Party that stood in Trowbridge and fought these issues? No. Did it have to be an organisation that paid allegiance for 40 years to Joseph Stalin? No. A determined left-wing Labour Party, as in Clay Cross in Derbyshire, might have done the job better. But that kind of principled Labour Party did not exist locally.

Without a doubt, Phyllis and Idris Rose cared about the town and its people more than the Trowbridge Labour councillors did. In the west Wiltshire context of a local Labour Party refusing to work with an effective and popular Communist Party, it was probably the case that only Phyllis and Idris Rose, with their commitment to Trowbridge workers, could have successfully raised socialist issues and materially helped them — for example by limiting rent rises.

What I would like to think is that some of the sons and daughters of the contemporaries of the Roses would be interested to find out more about them. We need to find Idris and Phyllis's daughter, if she is still alive, and grand-children if there are any. We need to talk to the surviving Trowbridge people who actually knew them.

In conclusion, I hope I have established that the story of Idris and Phyllis Rose is well worth acknowledging and preserving. I think their political achievements were considerable. Their contribution is an important part of the

Sources
Gradwell/Tuckett Papers, Swindon Trades Council files, Wiltshire and Swindon History Centre, Chippenham, Wiltshire Times files, Trowbridge Reference Library

---

Rosie MacGregor adds:

A retired Tory councillor, who asked not to be named, has said that whilst he would not advise us to put Idris Rose on a pedestal, he considered Idris to be a necessary challenge to the power held by the Conservatives in Trowbridge in particular two wealthy and influential families and their friends, who owned retail businesses and other premises in the area, they also held most of the power on the Town Council at that time.

Another rather sad story is told that after Idris died all his papers were destroyed.

Amongst those interviewed by Rosie were many who described him as a friend to those who would otherwise have had no voice, but there were some who suggested that Idris was not always the local hero and various rumours circulated about him, some of which seem improbable given his commitment to communism. What is certain is that a career in local politics can be a ruthless and competitive occupation. He was certainly a strong character who was loved by some but loathed by others. Whatever people thought of him, it cannot be denied that he was a man who could or would not be ignored.

Ted Poole from Swindon, a stalwart of the Communist Party, believed that Idris and Phyllis Rose suffered from misinformation put out by his opponents, Tories and Labour alike. Ted described Idris, who he knew very well, as 'a very loyal comrade who stood out like a beacon of light among the rest. Although he was not a bad speaker he was no firebrand. But he always had well thought out, very considered arguments. Idris never wavered in his support for the Labour movement nor for the Communist Party.'

The Swing Rebellion in Wiltshire

Nigel Costley, Regional Secretary, South West Trades Union Congress

It is quite shocking in many respects that so few people know of this story. One day whilst I was fact checking in Tidworth I knocked on the doors of some of the places involved just to check that we had identified the right place and I asked "do you know about the Swing?" And none of the people who lived in these places realised that 180 years ago — when riot, rebellion and uprising was the only way people could make their voices heard — a crowd of 400-500 people were banging on their doors and causing this rebellion that clearly rattled the authorities.

So what was the Swing Rebellion all about — what caused it?

The first issue was the enclosures, the seizing and enclosing of land that had previously been used by rural folk for their livelihood. The Western Rising in the 1600s broke out on the borders of Wiltshire, Somerset and Devon, which were covered in forests at the time. The rebellion was against the enclosures that took away the right to use the woodland for work. It affected the artisans whose means of survival relied on timber for their crafts.

The privatisation of land prevented local people from growing food and grazing their animals. The process continued throughout the Eighteenth Century.

By the 1830s, rural areas were suffering further hardship because of poor harvests. Unemployment had risen because the wars against France had ended and many people were brought back into the labour market at a time when the trade could not support it.

New corn threshing machines could do the work of ten men and they were the particular targets of rural people who blamed the machines for their plight.

The cloth trade, an important industry in this part of Wiltshire, was experiencing a series of new technologies that were forcing people out of work and reducing pay.

The industrial revolution was taking hold in all sorts of ways. The population was growing and the population was on the move. Traditional customs and ways of operating were falling apart. The Poor Law as a way of supporting people — the worthy poor at least — was coming apart at the seams.

Conditions in Wiltshire were particularly wretched and this was highlighted by William Cobbett, a great recorder and commentator of rural affairs in the 1800s.

In his book Rural Rides — his diary of riding around the countryside — he talked of Wiltshire as being a beautiful county, but he said, "this is, I verily believe, the worst used labouring people upon the face of the earth. Dogs, hogs and horses are treated with more civility". And he went on to warn, "the end will be dreadful". He wrote that in 1826. And he was not wrong. In 1831 the Swing Rebellion as we now describe it exploded across the south of Britain.

The combination of all these factors led ordinary working people into a situation of complete desperation where they had to find ways of fighting back. They had no vote and so really the only course was direct action.

This took different forms. It took the place of arson and burning ricks. It took the form of smashing machines. But it took other forms as well. In Wroughton near Swindon it took the form of smoking pipes in the cemetery — they really knew how to make an impact.

Captain Swing was a pseudonym for a fictitious character. People would write an anonymous letter to their employer with advance warning of what was to come saying "pay up, give us more money, or else" and the letter would be posted, signed Captain Swing.

I have a picture in my mind that late at night a group of blokes would gather around a hay rick trying to light a fire in poor conditions in the rain, but apparently the procedure was much more sophisticated and the fire raisers actually had to go out with sulphur lamps already prepared to light these fires.

Action sweeps from village to village

The arable farming carried out on the chalk lands sweeping across the southern half of Britain was particularly badly affected. Chalk is poor soil to grow things on especially before the advent of new fertilizers and grass strains. It is the clay of Gloucester and Devon that allows for dairy farming and cheese production.

This is where the expression "the difference between the chalk and the cheese" comes from.

But trying to draw a line in time around the Swing Rebellion is false because riots and rebellions were occurring before and after this period. Left is a picture of the time showing the desperation of the ordinary farm workers against the land owner.

Swing starts

One of the first incidents to take place in Wiltshire was at Knook where pea, barley, oat and bean ricks belonging to farmer Richard White were

burnt down and in Wilcot on 22nd November. On 23 November there was action taken at Pewsey, Wootton Rivers and Burbage. The contagion was spreading from village to village. The word was going out that this was the action to be taken.

So a threshing machine was destroyed at the farm of William Ferris who had threatened to shoot the crowd had they dared smash his machine. They ignored him anyway and in Wilton on 23 November 500 people, a combination of farm workers and mill workers in the town gathered to attack a mill of John Bishop.

A particularly nasty incident occurred at Pyt House just West of Salisbury. Warned of the approaching crowd, Mr Bennett of Pyt House rode out to meet some 400 people descending on his property.

A riot broke out when they arrived and stones were thrown, one striking Mr Bennett between the eyes.

The Yeomanry were called in. These were the land owners and the bigwigs who dressed up in uniform and marched out. In some parts of the Country the authorities could not actually trust the Yeomanry, so the forces of law and order were divided.

At Pyt House the Yeomanry were involved in what amounted to a pitched battle and John Harding, one of the rioters, was shot dead in that battle, the only fatal casualty in the Swing Rebellion certainly around Wiltshire. Other events took place throughout the local

villages and other machines belonging to Mr Bennet were smashed at Fontill Gibbon.

Charles Davis

Many people who rose to lead this rebellion will be forgotten. but we should do our best to remember them, people like Charles Davis who was born in All Cannings.

There were signs of the Swing Rebellion breaking out in All Cannings and Charles Davis was clearly involved in the activities. There are reports of men going around All Cannings and nearby villages, persuading others to join their demand for higher pay and the destruction of the threshing machines.

They met a man on horseback called Sir Edward Poor who urged them to disperse and warned them of the consequences of their actions. But he did have some sympathy for their plight and he gave them a sovereign and offered to meet them again and to mediate, although it is unclear whether he took his promise any further. The men continued to go from village to village gathering support. Crowds were getting bigger and the momentum of this occasion was clearly taking over.

A crowd of 300 men met at midday on 23rd November at the Rose and Crown in Woodborough. Charles Davis was elected or became — we don't quite know the process — the Captain, the leader of this crowd. And they marched towards Alton Barnes where they were aiming to smash the machine of a farm there. The initial arrivals, probably oiled with some beer from the pub at this point, banged on the door of the rectory of Reverend Augustus William Hale who claimed he met two half-drunken men who knocked on the door demanding money. He refused to give them

money at which point they marched off to the neighbouring farm belonging to Robert Piles. Reverend Hale in the meantime warned his wife to batten the hatches, bolt the doors, lock the windows and keep herself inside. Shortly afterwards the rest of the crowd started arriving and banging on the same door. She was clearly frightened and trying to disperse them she threw some shillings from the top window. They left her alone and went to join the others heading for Robert Pile's farm.

Robert Pile was a local bigwig and he was in Marlborough at the time — some reports say that he was selling sheep at the local market but others say that he was looking for Swing rebels elsewhere not knowing that they were attacking his farm.

About 50 men had already started to smash into his farm and look for his threshing machine. Interestingly, Charles Davis then spoke with the Reverend Hale and it sounds like quite a sensible argument. In fact the Reverend later said that no voices were raised. He described how, in good temper, he was involved in a discussion about the rights and wrongs of what they were doing and that Charles Davis explained that he thought it was legal to smash the machines because it was the machinery that was wrong and was breaking the order of things and it was within his rights to get rid of them. Davis said that the rioters were not involved in any arson and that he would hand in people who were caught raising fires.

An interesting quote, "We only wish that every man can live by his labour" indicates that the men could not survive with the appalling wages that they were facing and that direct action was the only course of action that they felt that they could take.

The Reverend rang the bells of the church to summon help, but it is recorded that only a few women and children arrived, and that was only from curiosity.

Robert Pile rushed back to his farm in a panic with pistol in hand, trying to disperse the crowd by firing over their heads. A kerfuffle took place and he ordered someone to get his shot gun. The Reverend went into the house and came back with a double barrelled shot gun and the crowd, fearing for their own safety, bundled him to the ground.

There was a melee with a large number of men set to destroy the machine and the farmer arrived, shooting at them. At some point Charles Davis was shot, but it is unclear exactly when. However, he intervened to protect Robert Pile and stop the mob from actually killing him. The double barrelled shot gun was smashed at some point and Robert Pile was at the mercy of the crowd. He would probably have been killed had it not been for Charles Davis and a man called Bullock who managed to drag him into his house for safety.

The crowd then smashed their way into the house still demanding money and the breaking of the machine. At some point whilst this was happening Mr Pile's sister lost £10 from her purse. But Charles Davis took responsibility to protect Mr Pile and his family and at this point the crowd eventually dispersed, some of them returning to the pub, where they apparently made merry with the money that they had acquired.

The troops were called out of Devizes. They arrested those in the pub and took them back to Devizes. A half-hearted attempt to rescue them led to more arrests.

The Devizes troop went back the next day, scouring presumably for Charles Davis and other leaders of the rebellion. They caught up and arrested him and took him to Bridewell gaol

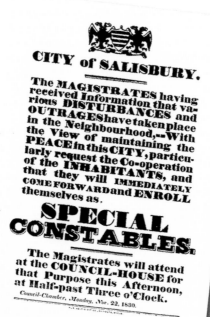

CITY of SALISBURY.

The MAGISTRATES having received Information that various DISTURBANCES and OUTRAGES have taken place in the Neighbourhood,—With the View of maintaining the PEACE in this CITY, particularly request the Co-operation of the INHABITANTS, and that they will IMMEDIATELY COME FORWARD and ENROLL themselves as.

SPECIAL CONSTABLES.

The Magistrates will attend at the COUNCIL-HOUSE for that Purpose this Afternoon, at Half-past Three o'Clock.

Council-Chamber, Monday, Nov. 22, 1830.

in Devizes.

How did the employers react to the riots?

Throughout the region, employers responded by holding meetings to discuss what they were going to do and raise funds to buy informers. There were some expressions of sympathy — rather patronising I think — for what they called the terrible plight of the working poor and occasionally some promise of maintaining the wages. The poster for the meeting at Warminster shows unveiled sympathy for the suffering of the working classes but calls for employers to resist their demands and to appoint special constables to sort it out.

Although the rebellion continued to sweep across Wiltshire and partly into Gloucestershire it did fizzle out and the authorities did get on top of the uprising.

A lot of people were arrested and many were taken to Salisbury.

Charles Davis was charged firstly with intent to destroy the house of Robert Pile. Reverend Hale gave evidence about the conversation he had with Charles Davis saying that their manner was not threatening and that he thought they were acting under the misapprehension that they were not breaking the law. Bullock gave evidence that Charles Davis assisted Mr Pile and kept the mob off as much as he could. So the court ruled that there was a failure to establish enough evidence against the prisoner and he was acquitted.

The next day he was charged with wounding Robert Pile. Evidence was given that actually Charles Davis was the one trying to protect Robert Pile even though at some point he actually himself got shot. He was acquitted.

So Charles Davis was then charged with robbing Mary Pile of the £10 out of her purse. Again evidence was given that Charles Davis far from actually robbing the sister was actually trying to get the mob out of the house. He was again acquitted.

The next day he was charged with destroying the threshing machine. At this point Davis said, "I'm very sorry, I was foolish as to go about breaking machines" and he was found guilty. He was also found guilty of an early affray against John Cliff. And the judgement of death was recorded. It was quite common for people to be sentenced to be executed — but few were.

On 7th February 1831 Charles Davis with 33 others was taken from Fisherton gaol to the York Hulk of Gosport to be transported to Australia for seven years. I don't know what happened to him afterwards and whether he made it home. Few actually did make it back home.

Summary

The Swing Rebellion consisted of four months of intensive protest. One person was killed at Pyt House by the authorities. The Swing Rebels didn't kill anybody. Physical violence against people was rare although there were lots of threats.

Although there were 252 death sentences, only 19 were actually hanged. A lot were transported including two women, including Elizabeth Parker from Gloucestershire. Most got between seven and 14 years' transportations, but very few came home because they had to pay their own fare to come home.

The average age of those arrested was 29 years. Half of them were married. Many more were imprisoned. Most were given a pardon after serving part of the sentence.

The squire covering the Dorset village of Tolpuddle accused two of the six farm workers arrested after the formation of an agricultural union of being involved in the earlier disturbances. There's no evidence for that, but it's hard to believe that they weren't aware and very conscious of the actual rebellion and the consequences. George Loveless realised that the Swing tactics had failed and he believed that the answer was not violence, smashing and arson but solidarity and trades union organising.

Chartism and rural workers in Wiltshire

by Steve Poole,
Reader in English Social and Cultural History at the University of the West of England and Director of its Regional History Centre.

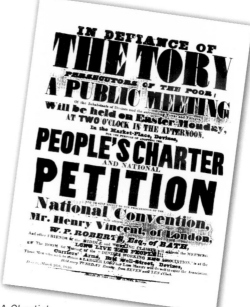

A Chartist poster advertising the second mass march to Devizes on Easter Monday, 1839. The intention to confront Tory power in its rural heartland is unmistakable — and in response the Mayor and magistrates of Devizes issued the poster below.

As interest gathered in making new 'histories from below' amongst socialist and labour historians during the 1960s and '70s, one of the first topics to attract detailed attention and new research was the Chartist movement.

Given Chartism's recognised status as the first nationally organised political movement of the British working class, this need not surprise us. Interest has continued to blossom. Alongside several new general histories of the movement, we now have a large number of monographs and essays on its leaders, its strategies, its means of communication, its women, its land-plan, its tea-totalism, its regional and local identity, its poetry and its press. Yet one area of Chartist politics still remains largely unexplored. Historians have been slow to come to terms with the association between Chartism, farm workers and the rural world. This may seem an odd omission, given that agricultural labour made up the single largest employment category of the period, but Chartism has most often been considered chiefly as a product of urban problems and historians have had some difficulty accommodating rural labourers' class consciousness. Significantly then, Adrian Randall's work on protest movements amongst rural Wiltshire's

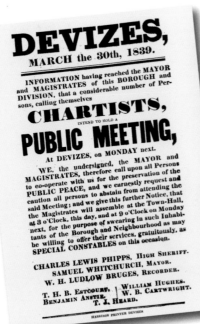

labouring communities in the 1830s and 40s has found no significant connection to urban Chartism.

How should we explain the relative failure of Chartism in rural Wiltshire? Parts of the county certainly produced very active Chartist associations, and it's clear enough that local leaders like Henry Vincent, William Carrier, William Roberts and the Potts brothers aspired to carry the Chartist mission into every corner of the county, particularly those rural areas bordering the industrial woollen towns of Trowbridge, Bradford and Melksham, and the semi-industrialised satellite villages of Bromham, Seend and

Holt.

Vincent, a journeyman print compositor who had come to the South West as a Chartist missionary from London, established a base at Bath in 1838 and was instrumental in the creation of several Chartist organisations in the Wiltshire towns. He was a platform speaker of rare ability, a consummate performer and an energetic organizer. And it was he who launched the first Chartist mission into agricultural Dorset where, despite interference from a number of mayors, landowners and magistrates, the reception was not unfriendly. In his own estimation, he scored a 'glorious victory over the parsons and farmers' of Blandford in November 1838 by attracting some 6000 people onto a nearby hill to hear him, 'a great portion of them being agricultural labourers who had come a distance of 20 miles'.

Resolutions were passed demanding higher wages for farm labourers but, although the usual format of open air meetings like these was for the Charter to be read and adopted, little reference seems to have been made to the conventional politics of the movement. It may be that the agricultural section of the audience had been attracted less by Vincent than by the freed Tolpuddle martyr, George Loveless, who shared the platform and pledged his assistance by accepting nomination to the upcoming Chartist Convention in London.

However, in appearing to back the Chartist mission, massing together in numbers and voting formally for resolutions, Dorset's labourers were breaking with the small-scale, inter-personal bargaining with employers with which they were more familiar, and their audacity drew swift reprisals from hostile farmers. Several were allegedly threatened with dismissal in the weeks following Vincent's visit, and with only the new Blandford workhouse for solace, and no Chartist networks in place to provide

Portrait of the West Country's best known radical missionary, Henry Vincent, made in 1842, shortly after his release from prison.

support, their interest quickly evaporated and no Chartist organisation was established. 'We can't expect them to starve for us', Vincent conceded a few weeks later.

Neither were difficulties like these peculiar to Dorset. As Roger Wells has shown, very similar problems beset Chartist missions to the countryside in the South East.

Making progress in Wiltshire proved equally difficult. Strength in the clothing districts was not reflected in the parishes bordering the important grain market of Devizes. A Tory town through and through, the party had secured both North Wiltshire county parliamentary seats in the keenly contested general election of 1837, and claimed one of the two borough seats the following year.

The county victory was particularly sweet for the Tories because they had enticed the erstwhile radical hero, Sir Francis Burdett (now a 'little renegade' in Vincent's opinion) to accept the nomination and, in so doing, believed they had symbolically swept reform from the regional political agenda.

It was revenge for the Reform Act of 1832, and for the Municipal Corporations Act of 1835, which between them had done much to blunt the electoral power of the landowning interest in the borough. The party's organ, the Devizes Gazette threatened violence against the first Chartist missionary to venture into the town, the Trowbridge cloth worker William Carrier. Carrier convened a small meeting in a public house but was rowdily interrupted. 'It was fortunate for him that he did not hold forth in the open street', mused the paper, 'or he might have regretted coming to Devizes'.

Twice in the Spring of 1839 Chartists tried to hold public meetings in the market place, but were on both occasions physically repelled by ad hoc armies of navvies and farm workers, marshalled by the farming interest and given the nod by magistrates and the under-sheriff.

Handbills circulated in advance by the 'friends of agriculture' had convened a farmers meeting at which it was deliberately resolved not to petition the mayor to veto the Chartist initiative. According to the Chartist Northern Star, one Farmer Brown of Horton was particularly active. 'Damn the mayor', he is supposed to have said, 'we can do it ourselves!' And they did. Fully expecting more trouble at the second attempt on Easter Monday therefore, many of the Trowbridge and Bradford Chartists who marched to Devizes were armed for their own protection. Vincent told the national Chartist leader, William Lovett, that they were going with 'sufficient force to put down the howling ruffians by whom we were previously assaulted', and Carrier was more combative still. They were going, he declared, not so much to hold a meeting of Chartists, but to 'meet the Tories'.

Peter Field
© 2011

Inevitably perhaps, rhetoric of this kind was interpreted by many in the farming region less as inter-party rivalry than as an attack upon the country by the town. For the Devizes Gazette, Chartism was just the latest in a long line of urban impositions upon rural social relations, and much was made of the non-local origins of the marching rank and file. They 'looked like factory workers', it was noted, not 'smock-frock men'.

And in the ensuing melee, it was the country that emerged triumphant. Vincent and Roberts, bloodied, bruised and beaten, blamed everything on the underhand tactics of the farmers. The 'poor labourers', they contended, condemned to ignorance and servitude by their tyrannical masters, had been charmed on the one hand by promises of new smocks, free beer or wage bonuses, and cowed on the other by threats of dismissal if they joined the Chartists.

Neither leader showed any sign of comprehending the urban/rural divide in more sophisticated terms than these, and offered no analysis beyond the one offered after the earlier setback at Blandford.

But there was no disguising the abject failure of the expedition, and its effects were quickly felt. It was now a simple matter for the Tories to consolidate their success by using the same strategy against another rural mission a week later, in the nearby village of Potterne. This time, it was alleged, the farmers simply offered their labourers payment of two shillings to 'drive the Chartists away'.

After all this, the Gazette was understandably satisfied that, despite the efforts of Chartist missionaries to turn their heads, most labourers remained 'well disposed'. The paper nevertheless advised local farmers to remind their workers of the most 'fearful retribution and ruin' meted out to them after the earlier Swing rebellion of 1830.

In the agricultural region, the anti-reforming climate of the post-1837 election years left Chartism looking considerably less relevant than it did in the manufacturing districts. In the eyes of a hostile county press, Chartists were little more than discredited liberals who wished, as one Devizes handbill put it, only to 'separate man and wife' with the draconian new Poor Law and to 'do away with agricultural labourers' altogether by lending support to the free traders of the Anti Corn Law League.

As Edwina Newman has shown, this charge was wide of the mark, for it is possible to trace considerable support for the League amongst organised farm labourers in Wiltshire during the 1840s.

Secondly, hostile propagandists were quick to saddle Chartism with the blame for the widespread practice of rural incendiarism. The firing of corn ricks and other kinds of farm property by workers exacting revenge upon unpopular masters had a lengthy lineage in the region's countryside; indeed it had been the predominant form of protest during the Swing uprising. But, seizing happily upon a remark of Carrier's that lucifer matches were cheap and easy to carry 'whilst out walking' in the countryside, a number of incendiary fires in farmyards were blamed by Tory newspapers on disgruntled Chartists from Trowbridge in the Spring of 1839. Trowbridge men were said to have 'openly gloried' over a fire at Keevil, and allegations of direct responsibility for encouraging incendiarists formed part of the evidence produced against Carrier at his later trial and conviction for sedition and conspiracy.

Although Vincent maintained that half of the three to four thousand men who turned out to hear him at Chippenham were agricultural labourers, and that when he called a meeting in Cirencester, 'the agricultural labourers poured in from the surrounding villages', in practice, urban agitators demonstrated little talent for engaging the rural world.

In a weekly 'Life and Rambles' column for his Western Vindicator newspaper, Vincent evoked the countryside frequently enough, but usually as a 'sweet', 'picturesque', 'delightful' or 'enchanting' backdrop to his political musings. He might occasionally stop in a village en route to an engagement in town, and convene a hurried meeting there in which to 'grease the farmers down'. He might equally encourage his rural readers to abandon their work in the fields and flock to the Chartist banner each time a march to an objective like Devizes passed their parish. But he expected only those few who were 'free from the trammels of the aristocrats' to have the nerve to do so.

The labourer's world was largely one of poverty and oppression to many Chartist propagandists, evoked in terms of outrage and pity and understood as a place apart. 'Heaven only knows', speculated the editor of the Regenerator in 1839, 'how many of our brave peasantry take with them into the fields cold boiled potatoes with an onion instead of meat, the water from the brook instead of beer, the cold grass turf for his table instead of the farmer's board...'

When Vincent addressed farm workers

"Pills for the Tories"

A woodcut from the Penny Figaro newspaper, 18 May 1839, depicts the arrest and interrogation of William Roberts, a radical Bath solicitor, second from left, and William Potts, a Trowbridge chemist. Potts, the short man with glasses had previously distinguished himself in the town by displaying bullets in his shop window labelled 'pills for the Tories'.

directly in print, he commonly adopted a tone more suggestive of a lecture to children than an approach to intelligent adults. 'To explain government properly to you', he wrote in an open letter to the labouring men of Potterne in June 1839, 'I shall liken it to something which you all understand. You all know what a farmyard is, because you generally work in or about such places'. He then compared the state to a farmyard and urged them to conclude, 'I'm dashed if I should not like to live in a well-managed farm of my own, receiving plenty of beef, bread, beer and bacon'. Adherence to the People's Charter, he assured them, would secure it for them.

Clearly, Vincent was no William Cobbett. By way of contrast, the 'cottage charter' promoted by Cobbett earlier in the decade had been equivocal over the Corn Laws for fear that if small farmers lost protection, they would transfer the burden by reducing the price of labour. For Cobbett, the repeal of the Game Laws was a more pressing issue for the rural poor, but Vincent had nothing to say about that.

Part of the problem, perhaps, was that mass platform politics and crowd action were an unknown quantity to most farm workers. It was true that during the Swing rebellion, labourers throughout Southern England had moved in small crowds from farm to farm, unmasked, and in broad daylight, but village politics in less extraordinary times were generally smaller in scale and either inter-personal or covert.

The feeling of some Chartists that men of 'more humble abilities' than Vincent would be better received was itself a suspicion that grand theatrical speeches about national affairs were not suitable for an audience accustomed to the specifics of local negotiation and community bargaining. In the years following Swing for instance, JPs in the Devizes region had responded with paternal and interventionist strategies aimed at reducing the rent charged to tenant farmers in return for increases in labourers' wages, and by this means a new deal of ten shillings a week was negotiated in 1831.

But it wasn't one-way traffic alone, and Vincent's belief that rural workers were too supine to organise in defence of their own

Peter Field © 2011

conditions was mis-judged. JPs who failed to support pay claims, who appeared as witnesses at the Swing Special Commission, or reneged on post-Swing wage deals were among the most common targets of incendiarism in the first half of the 1830s.

When nine separate arson outbreaks struck the region just as the Commission opened, JPs complained to the Home Secretary about the 'spirit of revenge prevailing amongst the peasantry', and a workforce that was 'infatuated and lawless'. 'I am sorry to say there is a disposition on the part of the farmers to reduce the labourers' pay', noted one Wiltshire JP in 1832, 'and assuredly as they do, there will be great rioting and an increase of burnings unless the magistrates in time increase the rate of relief to their families in proportion to the reduction'. Indeed, as average pay fell to eight shillings a week in November 1832, ricks were fired at Latton, Langford and Codford, prompting Lord Lansdowne to order the retention of the ten shilling rate at Bowood.

This pattern continued unabated during the Chartist years. Tut (piece work) was greeted at Urchfont by anonymous threatening letters in 1843 and £1400 worth of incendiary damage three years later. In the same parish, labourers successfully prevented cottage evictions three times between 1843 and 1849. And if discontent was focussed upon institutions of government, it was not so much parliament that attracted their attention, but the vestry and the Poor Law Union. 'We all went to the churchyard to see ourselves righted', said one man after blockading a vestry meeting at Christian Malford. 'Damn them all', asserted another, 'they deserve their ricks and their stacks to be burnt'! And so they were. There were at least six arson attacks around Bromham during the Spring of 1839 and another at Steeple Ashton was believed by the newspaper press to be yet another example of revenge for sackings imposed for attendance at Chartist rallies. Prompts like these did much to oil the wheels of paternalism.

Subverting the political economy of the new Poor Law, the Devizes Union maintained out-relief payments in 1838, in kind if not in cash. The effect was dramatic. During the last quarter of 1838, this Union relieved over two and a half thousand paupers, consigning only 305 to the workhouse, a practice it maintained into the 1840s. At Wilsford, where a ten shilling wage agreement was in place in1839, farmers also offered rent-free allotments to the poor, and in the vestry fixed out-relief payments to the sick at six shillings, a level just high enough to keep them from the workhouse.

Paternalism was not universal in Wiltshire at the end of the 1830s, but farm workers could be excused for believing that collective bargaining by incendiarism and negotiation was helping to keep political economy at bay. Their world was a complex one and a closed one, if the testimony of some outside observers is to be believed.

Barry Reay cites the American farmer Frederick Olmsted who visited rural England at the tail end of the 1840s and listened in on the conversations of farm labourers discussing the likelihood of revolutionary upheaval. 'It was strange what a complete indifference they all seemed to have about it', he wrote, 'as if they would be mere spectators, outsiders, and not in any way personally interested.

They spoke of the government and the Chartists and the landlords and the farmers, but not a word of themselves'. Olmsted thought them dysfunctional; beyond the reach of conventional politics, its structures and its concerns.

But Chartism's weakness was the inability of its leadership to address rural concerns in a relevant language, in an idiom that recognised distinctions between rural and urban experience, and to engineer solutions within a recognisable geography.

Rather than either lamenting the failure of rural Chartism or marginalising the agency of rural workers, historians might be better occupied examining the strategies of resistance that they did employ. For, as EP Thompson argued in his groundbreaking work on moral economy in 1970, acts of protest and resistance rarely conform to universal law and, particularly in rural culture, they remain phenomena that 'depended upon a particular set of social relations, a particular equilibrium between paternalist authority and the crowd'.

Further reading

The best modern accounts of the Chartist movement are Dorothy Thompson, The Chartists (London: Temple Smith, 1984) and Malcolm Chase, Chartism: A New History (Manchester: Manchester University Press, 2007). For Wiltshire see R. B. Pugh, 'Chartism in Somerset and Wiltshire' in Asa Briggs (ed.), Chartist Studies (London: Macmillan, 1959), and M. J. Lansdown, The Trowbridge Chartists 1838-1848 (Historical Association, West Wiltshire Branch, 1997). See also Roger Wells, 'Southern Chartism', Rural History, 2, 1 (1991), and Owen R. Ashton, 'The Western Vindicator and Early Chartism' in J. Allen and O. A. Ashton (eds.), Papers for the People: A Study of the Chartist Press (London: Merlin, 2005) for more on the regional context. An excellent recent textbook on rural social relations in the period is Barry Reay, Rural Englands: Labouring Lives in the Nineteenth Century (London: Macmillan, 2004). On rural protest in Wiltshire, see Adrian Randall and Edwina Newman, 'Protest, proletarians and paternalists: social conflict in rural Wiltshire, 1830-1850', Rural History, 6, 2 (1995).

Strikes and socialism in Swindon

The 1960s and 1970s

**by Derique Montaut,
Labour Party Leader, Swindon
Borough Council**

The 1960s and 1970s were very different from today. This was a time of industrial strife, when many wildcat strikes took place in the car industry and other factories. Shop Stewards in some firms were able to control recruitment, and were able to bring in political activists.

By and large shop stewards were not revolutionaries, nevertheless a number of left wing groups, including the Communist Party, tried to influence them with a political perspective. Some academics and left wing intellectuals even took unskilled factory jobs so they could preach dissatisfaction to fellow employees. MI5 were called upon by many employers to vet job applicants, and some operated on the shop floor.

Less than 10% of trades union members had any political affiliation, but we were prepared to support trades unionists in other companies in dispute with their employers by raising finance and helping with picketing.

Before I came to Swindon I knew nothing about trades unions or the left wing movement. I didn't come from a working class background. I don't have that heritage. I didn't have that passion. I was indifferent to everything that was taking place around me. I had been living in London, working as a laboratory technician in cancer research and as a young 20-year-old I had a child. I came from a middle class background but nevertheless I was struggling to exist. During that period the state of the world didn't affect me in any way because I was divorced from it. I just wanted to look after my family and get on with it.

I think I should start by explaining what was happening in Swindon before I arrived. Back in 1961 there was a mass strike at Pressed Steel over pay that lost, and a number of trades union militants were sacked, including Percy Jeffries, who later became a labour councillor, and who never worked in engineering again. I think he became an insurance salesman. The workers were forced back on lower pay than when they started.

In 1962 there was a national strike called by the Confederation of Shipbuilding and Engineering Unions over pay; the whole town was shut down, including the rail works. My first day at work was during that strike, and there was a picket on the gate. I explained that I had to go in, and they agreed to let me as long as I did no work, otherwise I would be sent to Coventry, so I walked through the gates and I started my training and induction.

The 60s was an interesting time. On the one hand there was the free love and the drugs — I had none of that — and on the other hand vast sections of the labour movement such as the docklands, operated a closed shop. And at the same time, local workers were objecting to the Afro-Caribbeans being brought into the country.

This was strange because they were taking the jobs the local workers would not do. There was prejudice. It was common in the London I had come from to see signs on pub doors saying "No blacks, no dogs, no Irish", always in that order.

I was able to get employment in Swindon, so I moved down. And I experienced a form of discrimination I hadn't experienced in London. Not racism in the sense of black and white, but as an attack on incomers from London.

The indigenous Swindon population took to the streets objecting to us newcomers taking their jobs and housing. However, we were only taking jobs the local populations wouldn't do and the housing was provided by funding from London County Council for these workers, not by Swindon Borough Council.

After I'd picked up some elementary skills the shop steward said, "You want a job, Jack, you join the union". And being a timid guy, I joined the union. I wanted to say to him that my name wasn't Jack, but I didn't have the courage to stand up to him.

I had some radical individuals around me. There were members of the Communist Party operating on the shop floor around me and there was a Maoist, although I don't think he

was a member. Politics was rife, everyone was discussing it and there were many heated words. It was a way of life, but I wasn't part of it. I just didn't want to know. In fact I hated and despised every part of what they stood for.

But things started to change after a while. I need to paint a picture of what it was like on the production line in the big Pressed Steel factory. We made the old British Leyland stampings and body parts, a body leaving the production line every few minutes. Pressed Steel when I started there, later Pressed Steel Fisher, was a private firm, aligned with the Morris Car Company. There were 7000 people working there, making panels for lots of different cars, including Jaguar and Rolls Royce.

We were working in very difficult situations where the Health & Safety Act and the Factories Act were not implemented. The environment was one of smoke and noise. The banging in the Press Shop sent many people stone deaf, as we had no ear defenders. Some parts of the factory were knee deep in dust, including asbestos, which we used in powder form and rubbed water into it by hand to use as putty in the welding areas. Sometimes we used to play with it like a toy.

Workers like myself were disking lead against

● **Braving the snow . . . Pressed Steel workers at their mass meeting.**

all the regulations. We were supposed to do this in a booth, but did it outside to save time. There was no enforcement and we regularly had lead poisoning, which led to six weeks off on the sick. When that happened we were moved off the lines and brought back once our blood levels fell back. At the end of the day you came out like a coal miner. Absolutely black. We took our breaks and had our food where we worked, in the dirt, because the canteen was too far away.

It was like this because we were a very young work force, mostly under 28. There were no women on the shop floor. And we were working on piece work, rather than measured day work. Piece work encouraged you to get more work done, but it also meant that when you had done enough you could knock off. Back then in the 1960s we were working a 30-hour week and the line workers at Pressed Steel were among the highest paid workers in the country.

There came a point when I had to stand up for myself in that environment. There was no other way to go. And when I started to stand up, the group around me recognised over a period of time that I was becoming a mouthpiece not only for myself but sometimes for them. And then I took on the shop steward's job. When I was elected as a shop steward I took the job for selfish motives. I didn't take the job on for them, but for me because I knew that the shop steward's job was a step on the progression into the management.

I was earning three times as much as I had in London. But the system meant that we were constantly negotiating over rates and it was prone to industrial action and consequently I became an industrial militant. And I found I was on the Economics League Blacklist. Back in the 60s we must have had a strike every day.

There were a lot of people around me who

SWINDON'S car men finally blew their tops today and brought the town's BL body plant to a standstill.

In two separate mass meetings this morning the plant's 3,000 members of the Transport and General Workers' Union voted to begin an indefinite strike.

By PAUL WILENIUS
Industrial reporter

Pickets sealed up the factory this morning and are stopping all heavy traffic moving in or out. Many branded the BL boss as Sir Michael "Adolf Edwardes."

Dozens of lorries carrying steel and car parts have been turned away.

After a mass meeting at 8.30 a.m. in a car park outside the factory 1,000 assembly workers went on strike.

They were followed a few hours later by the other 2,000 transport union men in the press shop and indirect workers.

lowed 12,500 other B.L. workers now on official strike over the pay deal.

Last straw

All the men on the Rover 3500 lines and the M.G. body production walked out in support of the Triumph TR7 assembly workers who were laid off indefinitely last night without pay.

Derek Montant, a senior assembly worker shop steward, said today: "The assembly workers are not prepared to accept an offer which will mean a cut in their living standards. This is the straw that broke the camel's back."

Gauntlet

All production at the body complex is now at a standstill.

The local Transport Union leaders received official blessing for the strike from the National Union leader, Grenville Hawley, this morning.

There will be a further mass meeting of the night shift workers at the Gorse Hill recreation ground tonight, and all 3,000 Transport Union strikers will meet again on Friday morning.

Jimmy Pitt, leader of the assembly workers, said today: "Sir Michael Edwardes has thrown the ... and we ...

● EVERYTHING was back to normal at Westinghouse Davenset Rectifiers, Chippenham, today after yesterday's mass walkout of most of the workers.

About 250 stopped work at lunchtime, and spent most of the afternoon at a meeting with full-time union officials in the Neeld Hall.

They are angry at the decision to move the unit out of Chippenham to Leicester where a new ... is being built.

saw trades unions in more political terms. During the 1960s and 70s there was a group of people within the Labour Party and probably within the Communist Party taking the parliamentary road to socialism.

Some others thought that there was going to be a working class revolution; but the left wing movement was very fragmented and there were many Marxist groups operating within the working class, including the International Marxist Group, the Socialist Labour League, which then became the Revolutionary Workers' Party, and a number of anarchist groups. People had moved to Swindon from strong union backgrounds, from the docks, the mines and the print, and they would talk about socialism.

All these other people around me started to have an influence on my behaviour. I started to develop like other trades unionists and I started to think about other people and other families. I started to take on a political perspective. I became the leader of the production side of the National Union of Vehicle Builders. It was the largest motor industry union and dominated the industry. It subsequently amalgamated with the Transport & General and is now a member of Unite, which I'm currently a member of.

Back in those days we didn't have ballots for strikes. Meetings took place to decide what industrial action we would take. I had a loud speaker in my car and shop stewards had loud hailers. Very many strikes took place and I soon became the deputy senior shop steward, then senior shop steward and became the leading light in the plant.

People trusted me to make the call. If I signalled that we were on strike, then all work stopped, and that was our power in negotiations. People wanted to be associated with me and the union, and when I walked down the line to meet management I would be flanked by an entourage of heavies.

Special Branch used to have people in the plant, and occasionally the police would let me know they had an eye on me.

The position of shop steward was highly sought after. It wasn't a question of saying, "I'm the best one for the job, I want it". There was competition. There were a lot of people within the left struggling for leadership of the working classes.

Although there was mass involvement in the union, and we had factory gate meetings of thousands, very few attended branch meetings. Perhaps only 10 or 12 people came to NUVB branch meetings, and many of them had to as they collected subs by cash. But there was a group of activists. We had a huge banner that needed eight people to carry. It said "Nationalise the Motor Industry under workers control", and we took it everywhere. I was on picket lines right round the country.

Because of my militancy on the shop floor I was picked up by the Socialist Labour League (now the Workers Revolutionary Party). We thought they were going to lead a British revolution. We looked at the Communists as Stalinists and every other revolutionary as a betrayal of the Marxist ideology. That's how fragmented the left was at that stage in fighting for those ideals.

The SLL was quite important in Swindon, with leading union activists in the rail works, Pressed Steel and Deloro Stellite. Tankie Howell was AEU District Secretary, and Frank Willis a convenor at the rail works was a prominent figure in the town. I was a sponsor for him standing as the Young Socialist candidate in the 1969 Swindon by-election, and I joined the party around that time.

For our regular branch meetings we only had about seven or eight attending, but they were prominent trades unionists, and for big public meetings we could get far more. The SLL leader, Gerry Healy, often used to come to Swindon. He was the most marvellous orator. I have never

heard the like of him since.

My own relations with SLL were strained from the beginning. They described me as a bit of a "reformist" because they were always pushing for a general strike and I wasn't prepared to gamble the real strength we had built up gradually. I had bought into the idea of a revolution, but knew what we could and couldn't deliver in the here and now.

The Communist Party were also influential in

● Dialogue of doom? . . . Union leader Derek Montaut on duty outside the Pressed Steel factory at Stratton yesterday.

Swindon at the time, and got quite big votes in the Parks ward, and there was a strain with the SLL because I sometimes supported them.

Although there were political activists in the plant, most workers there were limited to a trades union vision. The militancy was in the unskilled and semi-skilled grades. At that time the skilled fitters in the more moderate AEU actually earned less than us. But while people were very willing to use industrial muscle for local issues, and to defend local conditions; if there was a national vote for a strike, but Swindon had voted against, it was hard to get them out.

I remember on one occasion we announced there would be a national strike, though Swindon had voted against; and a big Scottish bloke came up to me and very threateningly said "Who the fuck do you think you are", and threatened to break my legs. I think he meant it. On the day, we had a picket, but about 300 gathered on the other side of the road and they charged the gates. It was nose to nose confrontation, but in the end most of them respected the strike, and only a few dozen went in.

At that time full-time officials to some extent were seen to be no better than the management because they were always trying to counsel people to go back to work; and the unions had a tension with the rank and file plant officials. I remember Frank Chapple of the Electricians unions having a meeting in the old Town Hall where he read out a list of militants that he didn't want in his union.

The Workers Revolutionary Party claimed to represent about 15,000 people at one stage. The young Derique Montaut was regularly seen going into the pubs with his Workers Press and selling it on the factory gates. But the Labour Party was the more dominant and we struggled for positions within the Trades Union movement. I found it difficult after a period of time to sustain my position in the Workers Revolutionary Party. I had a quota of "Workers Press" papers to sell in the plant, and the heavy sacrifices of time and money were hard for a family man like me.

Consequently, whilst I continued in my role as a plant convener, I eventually joined the Labour Party. It wasn't easy to leave the SLL, it almost felt like a divorce. I leave it to other people to determine whether I sold out. But a lot of Labour members in Swindon Borough Council also came from very similar backgrounds.

During that period there were many strikes in

the British Leyland group. Red Robbie wasn't considered within the shop steward movement to be the radical militant that he's sometimes painted out to be although he was sacked for what he stood for. The failure on our part to give him support was terrible but that's how it happened. He was sacked on a pretext because BL wanted to make an example of him.

Michael Edwards, a South African business man, was brought in to rescue the company, and he started a "year zero" and ripped up all previous agreements. There was a national strike, but we lost, in the end in Swindon there were just two of us out, myself and Eric Smith, who also later went on to become a Labour councillor and mayor.

The miners' strike in itself presented us with all kinds of problems. We had collections and we raised large sums of money for the miners, but to some extent the Labour Party under Neil Kinnock's leadership betrayed the miners in as much as they didn't support it. When I met Neil Kinnock I told him that in my opinion he had failed to support the miners and he said it was Scargill that had let down the miners. We agreed to differ.

Our militancy couldn't last because it was all based on assumptions of endless growth and profitability. It was fair weather trades unionism, when we were pushing against an open door; and the car industry set the norms for all of engineering.

There was a crisis of international capitalism in the 1970s, and there was over-production of cars. The employers had very little option, they had to change.

It's no idle threat

THE Right - To - Work campaign was launched in Swindon last night.

It will take the form of meetings and protests throughout the summer, culminating in the march of the unemployed through Swindon.

Hundreds of jobless youngsters from South Wales will march right through Wales and the South West picking up more unemployed marchers along the way.

They will arrive in Swindon on September 30, and will organise meetings and demonstrations before setting off for the Tory Party conference in Brighton the next day.

Jarrow

John Deason, the national organiser, of the march, told a meeting at the Co-op Hall in East Street last night that delegations will be sent to factories throughout the town.

"We will organise factory gate meetings, lobbies of workers, and meetings all over the town to protest a~ ~mas-

By PAUL WILENIUS
Industrial reporter

sive unemployment in the country," said Mr Deason.

"This is part of the battle of ideas against the Tories, who are now trying to permanently change the society we live in."

The economic crisis is so serious — even in Swindon — said Labour councillor Derek Montaut, that we are going back to the days of the Jarrow marches.

"The recession is here to stay. But it is making very real human tragedies for the people thrown out of a job.

"We now have people queueing up to get voluntary redundancy, but they are giving away jobs which are not theirs to give away."

The bad weather kept the turnout at the meeting down to about 40, but a committee has been set up to organise the reception for the Right-to-Work marchers.

They started to play us off against each other, not only between different countries, but also plant against plant; the TR7 was moved down to Swindon from Liverpool because BL thought they could do it cheaper here. I argued for blacking it, but it wasn't a popular argument, because people wanted the jobs.

The industry suffered from lack of investment, poor industrial relations, the fact that BL had too many models and too poor quality, and there was a sense of complacency that whatever happened the British motor industry would survive and we would keep our jobs. In honesty, the unions did our part to perpetuate the problems and resist changes that were needed. We didn't trust management, and resisted everything they did, and they have to share the blame for that for their own confrontational attitude.

Piece rates were done away with by a process of job evaluation, which had been one of the recommendations of the Donovan Commission. This reduced militancy and for the first time the skilled workers earned more than us. The unskilled were bought off with a lump sum.

In 1991 I gave a presentation called "Rover Tomorrow" to about 200 Rover managers, putting forward a blue-print for how they could improve their side of industrial relations, confide more with the trades unions and take input from the staff side on their plans, as we all share an interest in job security and improving conditions.

Industrial relations did improve after BL was sold to British Aerospace, and they brought in collaboration with Honda, which was a good hope for the company, as we had joint product development, team working and better quality. But then British Aerospace went behind Honda's back to sign a deal with BMW, and all that stopped, and BMW had a more autocratic management style.

Today Trades Unions are not able to defend their right to take the industrial action that we used to. And the consequence of that is frustration, and the membership of Trades Unions now is nowhere near the level in the 60s and 70s. Although in some ways trades unions have become cleverer at what they do.

While you might be critical of the way we acted I would defend our position robustly. We did what we had to do in the conditions of the time and we used the tools we had. We achieved the highest level of wages, we defended our people, we didn't betray them and consequently we kept organised labour in control.

The Trowbridge Martyr

Picture by Bob Naylor

Thomas Helliker's tomb in St James Parish Churchyard in Trowbridge

Thomas Helliker and the Wiltshire outrages of 1802

**by Prof Adrian Randall,
Birmingham University**

Thomas Helliker (or Hilliker or Elliker, the spelling of his name varies across documents and across time) was born in 1783, the second youngest of eight sons of Thomas and Elizabeth Hilliker. His elder brothers, John, Robert and Joseph were all apprenticed as shearmen and his younger brother James, like Thomas, followed in their footsteps. Thomas began his apprenticeship in 1797, working for Thomas Naish in his workshops in the Conigre, already a slum corner of Wiltshire's principal cloth-making town, Trowbridge.

Shearmen, or croppers as they were called in Yorkshire, were the labour aristocrats of the woollen industry since their role involved high-level skill and judgment. They occupied a pivotal point in the production of woollen cloth, taking the material once it had been woven and fulled and then first raising a nap by brushing the surface of the cloth with a 'handle', a cross-shaped wooden tool set with teazle heads, before shearing it flat with large hand shears.

All cloths had to be raised and sheared many times in order to produce the soft even texture which was the pride of the industry and which commanded premium prices. The quality of their work determined the final value of the cloth: it was said 'They can make a piece 20 per cent better or worse by due care and labour or the reverse.'

Most, in the West and in Yorkshire, were employed in workshops owned by master dressers or master shearmen and the culture of the workshop was that of independent craftsmen.

A correspondent to the Leeds Mercury in 1803 said of the Yorkshire croppers:

"A cropper strictly speaking is not a servant. He does not feel or call himself as such, but a cloth worker, and partakes much more of the nature of a shoemaker, joiner, taylor, etc ... Like them, he comes and goes, stops a longer or shorter time ... according as he may chance to work."

Shearmen earned good money: croppers in 1812 were said to be able to spend 'twice or three times as much money at the ale house than the weaver or dyer' and their West Country colleagues enjoyed similar incomes. Shearmen ranked among the elite crafts in their localities.

In 1797 when Thomas took out his indentures there was little indication that those who were responsible for finishing the finest woollen cloth produced in the country would themselves be finished before a lad like him might reach middle age.

The years before Thomas's birth had witnessed extensive conflicts over the introduction of spinning and scribbling machines into the Wiltshire woollen industry. As he grew up, the beginnings of a factory system were slowly emerging. And as he set out to learn his trade, that too was coming under threat from the gig mill and the shearing frame. The gig mill, essentially a series of revolving linked rollers, each set with teazles, across which the fulled cloth was drawn, was a crude but cheap way of raising the nap. Powered by horse, water or steam, it threatened craft jobs. It was far from a new invention.

It, or something like it, had been around in the mid-sixteenth century when it was proscribed by the statute, 5 & 6 Edward VI, c. 22, 'An Act for the putting down of gig mills'. Cloth dressers had long been willing to accept its use on coarse white cloth, but they were not prepared to tolerate its extension to finer cloths, the mainstay of both regions' economies.

The second threat came from the shearing frame, invented by a Sheffield clergyman, John Harmer, in 1787 and then improved in 1794.

It was made up of pairs of shears set in a frame which was drawn across the cloth while the shears were operated mechanically. A new invention, it was not covered by the old legislation.

Between them, these two machines foretold the demise of the dressers' trade.

Wiltshire shearmen had no intention of tolerating either.

Back in 1767 a clothier in the village of Horningsham had attempted to set up a gig mill, assuming that its distance from the main woollen towns would provide adequate protection.

Over 500 shearmen assembled from across the region, marched on the village and destroyed it.

That put off most clothiers until 1795 when the machine reappeared, this time in a mill just outside Marlborough. Too far away for direct action, the Wiltshire shearmen turned to the law.

At the summer assizes of 1796 they brought a prosecution against the manufacturer, Samuel Cook, 'for using a gig mill contrary to 5 and 6 Edward VI'.

It was dismissed on a technicality but the Wiltshire shearmen remained convinced the law was on their side. However, the case persuaded them that direct action would be a more effective weapon.

So, when in 1797, the firm of Bamford and Cook set up not only gig mills but also shearing frames in their mill at Twerton, near Bath, 2-300 men assembled.

They marched first to Nunney where they forced their way into a shear grinder's shop where Bamford's shears were being sharpened and smashed them and then, their number strengthened to, it was claimed, 8-900, marched on to Twerton 'in order to hang up Bamford and two of his men, to burn down his works and those of Collicott and Co'.

Only their timely interception by the magistrates, backed by cavalry, prevented them achieving their intention.

Other clothiers who set up gig mills at Batheaston had their property attacked. Thomas, the new apprentice, would certainly have known all about these assaults.

The threat from machinery led the cloth dressers to establish a national federation, called the Brief Institution, in 1797.

Based in Leeds, the Institution united all cloth dressers across the country in one union with a common structure and a common membership card, depicting crossed shears over the motto, 'May industry & freedom unite us in friendship'.

Helliker's older brothers, out of their apprenticeship, were certainly members and his eldest brother, John Helliker, became an elected member of the Trowbridge shearmen's committee.

The Wiltshire Outrages

For a few years the main textile towns of Wiltshire saw no gig mills. But in April 1802, two Warminster clothiers, fearing the undercutting of their trade by producers in Gloucestershire where gig mills were increasingly used, took the plunge. The result was an explosion of industrial conflict, known as the Wiltshire Outrages.

Henry Wansey and Peter Warren introduced gig mills. Their shearmen immediately stuck work.

As the strike progressed, their property came under attack. First, both men received anonymous threatening letters. Then minor pieces of property were destroyed: a row of young trees was cut down and a hayrick set on fire.

The strike soon extended to other dressing shops around. When clothiers elsewhere started to send their cloths to the Warminster gig mills to be dressed, further disorder occurred.

The cart of Mr Bayley of Calstone Mills near Devizes, returning from Warminster loaded with cloths, was overtaken on the Downs by six men with blackened faces who took out the cloths, cut five or six of them to pieces and damaged fourteen others to the amount of £200.

More damage followed. Warren lost a rick of

oats, a large dog kennel and, a fortnight later, a barn and stable. Troops were rushed to the town and the clothiers held firm.

The Warminster clothiers' lead encouraged others to try out gig mills. Clothiers in Trowbridge and Bradford on Avon, still deterred by the powerful shearmen, baulked at this but they combined to use the threat of the machines to reduce the time allowed for manual finishing of cloths, in effect forcing down wages. Their shearmen immediately went on strike. The biggest threat to the shearmen, however, was posed by the new large mill erected in 1801 by John Jones at Staverton. The 'Staverton Superfine Woollen Manufactory' epitomised a future which woollen workers across the region dreaded. Standing 'not less than six different floors and having sixty five window to the front', the mill was 'filled with every sort of newly invented machinery so that every kind of process except weaving can be done there.' From its completion it had attracted hostility: Jones, a magistrate, wrote to the Home Office demanding further troops to protect it and to intimidate refractory workmen. The striking shearmen had persuaded many of Jones' workers to join them, 'under a pretence that they had been threatened and forced to do it'. It was, he claimed, 'a most wicked attempt to ruin our manufacture by threats'. Jones responded by introducing shearing frames, thereby exacerbating the conflict. The immediate result was an attack on the mill. Windows were smashed but the attackers seem to have been driven off by armed guards. A further two companies of infantry were now rushed to the area specifically 'for the purpose of assisting the magistrates by acting as sentries or guards upon sundry mills'.

The military presence did not prevent further destruction. The following night a mill and house owned by John Newton at Clifford were set on fire and burned down. Other attacks followed. And on the night of 22 July a mill at Littleton, near Semington, owned by a Trowbridge clothier, Francis Naish, was burned down. Naish, a man who had risen from being a master dresser, had bought the old corn mill in 1797 and converted it for spinning. It seems

likely that in 1802 he erected finishing machinery there. The mill was managed by Ralph Heath who lived near the premises. Along with three workers, he had been guarding the mill every night for weeks. That evening Heath, waiting in his cottage, received a message from Naish that he had heard the shearmen might attack that night. Heath had hoped for soldiers but none

Peter Field © 2011

were sent. At about one o'clock 'four or five men, some with their faces blacked and all of them Armed with Muskets, Pistols, Bayonets and other weapons Rushed into the Room crying out "Stand you Buggers", at the same time presenting their arms and swearing "that no one should stir".'

Their leader demanded, 'Damn your eyes, is there any soldiers or guards here?' and, not trusting Heath's denial, went out to check, leaving one man, with 'his face blacked and a pistol in his hand', standing guard on Heath and his assistants. The mill was set on fire and burned to the ground at a loss said to run to £8,000.

The destruction of the mill broke the nerve of the Trowbridge clothiers who abandoned their attempt to force down wages. The shearmen returned to work and 'afterwards printed and circulated a paper of what had been agreed to. However an attempt at open negotiation with Jones failed and a delegate announced 'he would rather be hanged than recommend to the shearmen to accept Jones' offer'. The result was a second attack on Staverton. This time a brisk fire fight broke out as defenders sought to drive off attackers who scaled the high surrounding walls, clearly with every intention of entering the premises. A bell summoned dragoons who had been stationed nearby in the expectation of trouble but, though they spent the next hour scouring the neighbourhood, they caught no one. The following night a dwelling house owned by Jones at Bearfield was set on fire and destroyed. Jones believed it was a ruse to draw off the mill's defenders to enable a third attack but the soldiers did not leave their posts.

The attacks on the mills frightened most clothiers into abandoning their use of the gig mill. Direct action had worked. But the successful attack on Littleton mill came at a price. Heath, Naish's employee, subsequently claimed to have recognised the man who had stood guard over him as Thomas Helliker. Under Naish's prompting Helliker was arrested and immediately incarcerated in Fisherton gaol, Salisbury. That night, Naish's workshops in Trowbridge burned to the ground.

The Wiltshire Outrages outraged the government. Convinced that the local magistrates were showing too little resilience in the face of disorder, they had dispatched more troops and, crucially, a Bow Street magistrate, James Read, to the county to take charge of counter-measures. He set in train a policy of continual harassment:

'Two or more justices meet daily at one or other of the manufacturing towns, and as the Combination Acts afford a very convenient pretext for summoning and examining upon oath any suspected persons, I have continually some before them. It answers the double purpose of keeping the magistrates at their post and of alarming the disaffected.'

Displaying scant regard for legal niceties, a model which would be followed by magistrates in Yorkshire in 1812, Read arrested many shearmen, often merely on suspicion, and sent them to Salisbury gaol in the hope that, far from their friends, they might talk. He had high hopes that Thomas Helliker, the only one positively identified, would impeach others but the youth resolutely maintained his innocence and said nothing about the outrages. In August Read did manage to get details about the Brief Institution

from one shearman, Thomas Bailey, and was able thereby to seize the union's books and arrest the committee. All were thrown in prison until the assizes in March the following year, John Helliker among them, charged with 'aiding and assisting at, and present at, and consenting to, the administering or taking an oath or encouragement, by James May of Trowbridge, clothworker, to the said Thomas Bailey.' Bailey, their accuser, was also kept in prison, in Marlborough bridewell, 'for the protection of his person as that may be forthcoming when wanted'.

At the assizes in March 1803 the first case heard was that against the Trowbridge shearmen's committee. But, in spite of having being kept in quarantine, the state's one witness, Thomas Bailey, was got at. His 'recollection failed him ... And on account of the oath not being proved ... the prisoners were acquitted.' The prosecutors were furious. Of the shearmen, only Thomas Helliker remained for trial. We can but wonder at the feelings of John, freed but now watching his young brother stand trial for his life.

His hopes may have been bolstered because he would have known that his brother had an alibi. This was to be provided by Thomas' friend and fellow apprentice, Joseph Warren. Like Thomas, he had worked for Naish at the Conigre. In his deposition to the Trowbridge magistrates made two days after Thomas's arrest, Warren claimed that the two had been out on the town drinking on the night on which the mill at Littleton was attacked. Helliker, he claimed, had been so drunk that he was unable to get home and so Warren had helped him into the kitchen of the house belonging to John Walter, where Warren was staying. Warren had a 'sweetheart', Ann Walter, presumably the reason for his stay. Warren claimed to have locked Helliker in the kitchen, putting the key in a place of which Helliker, lost in a drunken stupor, could not have known. Only when morning came and Walter rose to unlock the house could Thomas have got out. It was not much of an alibi but, as long as Warren and Walter were prepared to swear in court that it was true, it might well secure Thomas's acquittal.

As soon as he heard of this deposition, his employer, Joseph Naish, immediately 'interviewed' the boy. He had reason to be worried. His millman, Ralph Heath, had positively identified Helliker. Now that one positive connection stood in jeopardy. But before he could investigate further, Warren disappeared, spirited away by the shearmen to Yorkshire. They realised that once James Read, the Bow Street magistrate, learned of this new evidence, he would arrest Warren and grill him, as he did other suspects. The flight north does not suggest that the shearmen were confident that Warren's alibi would stand.

We do not know what his evidence might have achieved because Warren never turned up for Thomas Helliker's trial. We do, however, know that it was expected by all that he would. His sweetheart, Ann Waller, wrote to him, '1 know that you cannot come to me unless you do mean to involve yourself in trouble and put it out your power to do anything for your friend.' She urged him to be careful with his money, 'for you will not be sure to have work till the time you must come home which will not be till March next.' The assizes were set of March 1803.

Warren's uncle was William May, another member of the shearmen's committee and brother of James May, the secretary. William was a trusted figure in the union and served as an envoy from the Wiltshire men to Yorkshire in December 1802 when the respective costs of employing a counsel for the forthcoming parliamentary enquiry into the industry were agreed. William wrote to Joseph Warren: 'you must not come here by no means. There was a report that you were seen at Beckington, but I knew better but let it go, so much the better that they are ignorant.'

However, the authorities were not ignorant. These letters were intercepted and forwarded back to Read in Wiltshire. They probably had been sent via George Palmer, a Leeds shoemaker, who acted both as post box and agent for the union. His involvement was discovered, probably by the Leeds magistrate and merchant, William Cookson, during the course of the Wiltshire Outrages. Thereafter, all correspondence going to Palmer was routinely intercepted and read.

Did Joseph take fright and simply stay in Yorkshire? This seems unlikely since the Yorkshire croppers would have known who he was and the key role which he was destined to play. Moreover, he could only have found work in the cropping shops with their blessing. It is distinctly possible, therefore, that he was prevented from returning by agents of the state. His absence probably sent Thomas to the gallows.

Yet others had the power to save Helliker with far stronger testimony than that which Warren might have offered. As noted, Heath had three servants with him on the night of 22 July 1802. One of them, John Pearce, made a statement soon after the attack. It contradicted in several ways that testimony given by his employer. According to Heath, the men who had rushed into the cottage had all been armed, the leader carrying a musket, Helliker, the second man to enter the room, carrying a pistol and the rest carrying an assortment of firearms. Heath also stated that the men, including Helliker, had their faces blackened. When cross-examined at the assizes, Heath claimed that Helliker's face had still been recognisable, even though it was blacked. When asked why it had taken him several days before he identified Helliker, he stated that he had not identified him straightaway 'from a dread that his life was in danger if it had been understood that he could convict him'. This was a plausible explanation.

Pearce's deposition, however, made shortly after the attack and before that of Heath, stated that only one man, the 'short' man who had entered first and who was plainly the leader, had a blackened face or carried a pistol; the rest, he deposed, had their coats pulled up to disguise themselves and carried bayonets fixed on poles. This contradiction suggests at least some question as to Heath's memory. Heath had been keen to present himself in an heroic light. When the men left, he had, he claimed, immediately followed to see if he might save the mill, but had been ordered back inside. Later, 'at the hazard of his life', he had managed to save some cloths before the conflagration overwhelmed the building. Pearce's testimony stated otherwise. According to him, when the shearmen declared that they intended to burn the mill, Heath had replied, 'burn it down or let it stand. We can't hinder you, if you burn it down I shall sleep in peace which I have not done

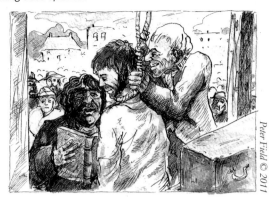

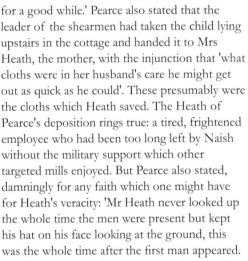

Peter Field © 2011

for a good while.' Pearce also stated that the leader of the shearmen had taken the child lying upstairs in the cottage and handed it to Mrs Heath, the mother, with the injunction that 'what cloths were in her husband's care he might get out as quick as he could'. These presumably were the cloths which Heath saved. The Heath of Pearce's deposition rings true: a tired, frightened employee who had been too long left by Naish without the military support which other targeted mills enjoyed. But Pearce also stated, damningly for any faith which one might have for Heath's veracity: 'Mr Heath never looked up the whole time the men were present but kept his hat on his face looking at the ground, this was the whole time after the first man appeared.

Pearce was seemingly never asked to confirm his draft statement, neither was he nor the other two servants who had shared the ordeal called to give testimony at Helliker's trial. The sole witness for the prosecution was Heath. He confidently stated that 'he verily believes that the said Thomas Hilliker to have been a ringleader and Principal in the offence'. With a £500 reward nestling in his pocket this was no time to suggest uncertainty.

Heath's testimony condemned Helliker. Thomas's counsel, a Mr Garrow, who had been 'engaged on a special retainer, with Messrs Jekyll and Borrough', itself evidence of the continuing financial strength and resolution of the shearmen to save their young colleague, tried hard to find weaknesses in Heath's evidence. He 'endeavoured to show that as the men who entered the factory were disguised, it would be impossible for anyone to know their features; and he examined Mr Heath whether he had not

confessed that he could not swear to the prisoner.' Heath stuck to his story. It was the rock on which the defence was to founder. The Salisbury and Winchester Journal reported:

'The jury deliberated for about ten minutes, during which time Helliker was in great agitation. When at length they pronounced him guilty, he appeared as if relieved from a torturing suspense, and to assume a degree of fortitude to encounter his fate and which he retained when the sentence of death was pronounced. He is a good looking youth, only nineteen years old. He is left for execution.'

Thomas Helliker was left to languish for a week before the execution, during which time frantic efforts seem to have been made to secure a reprieve. They were in vain. On 22 March 1803, he was taken from his cell to the gallows outside the prison at Fisherton. Even the press which had condemned the shearmen's campaign of violence could not forebear some sympathy for the boy.

'Hilliker, ere this, bore a fair character for his station in life, and after his conviction his behaviour was decent and resigned. At the scaffold he betrayed neither unmanly fear nor audacious daring. His youth, and his falling a victim to a party, caused much commiseration for his fate; but the object in which he had been engaged, followed, as it generally is, with violence, anarchy, and misery, prevented the success of powerful applications in his behalf; since a severe example was necessary to put down such illegal combinations.'

His body was placed on a cart and brought back across the chalky tracks of the empty unenclosed Wiltshire plains, echoing to the sounds of sheepbells and skylarks. As the cart left the upland 'chalk' and descended to the 'cheese' of the vale, passing through the textile-making villages, a procession gradually formed the funeral cortege and, before reaching Thomas's home town of Trowbridge, it was, it was said, met by a large number of girls, dressed in white who provided an honour guard for the dead boy. An 'immense' crowd, their number swelled by representatives of the Yorkshire croppers, insisted that Thomas would be buried in the churchyard of the large parish church of St James. The vicar was absent and the curate was compelled to bury Thomas with full Christian rites. There his body lies to this day, since the attempts of the returning vicar to disinter him were firmly resisted.

Was Thomas innocent?

Certainly the legal case against him was critically flawed. His prosecutors knew of Pearce's deposition but ignored - or buried - it. Thomas was earmarked to be the 'severe example' the state required. They were not to be denied their victim.

But might he have been there at Semington? Yorkshire Luddites did occasionally have lads under 21 in their midst. But these were at large-scale assaults on mills where numbers were needed. The group at Littleton was small, necessary to enable them to elude the dragoons. It is unlikely that they would have taken an apprentice who was not a full member of the Brief Institution. There was also a real risk of recognition for anyone working for Naish in attacking Littleton. Heath would know them well. On balance it seems very unlikely Thomas was there.

So why did Naish have him arrested? It is probable that Thomas, brother of three full members of the Brief Institution including

Peter Field © 2011

Committee member John, knew who had been there. Perhaps it was his brother Joseph, to whom special reference is made in the letter Thomas is said to have written from gaol. Perhaps he inadvertently let slip this knowledge or hinted at knowing something when at work and in the hearing of one of Naish's foremen. Whatever it was, he was not taken up at first with being at the mill but on suspicion of knowing who was there. From that point on, the evidence was focused, deliberately and with malice, against him.

In this respect, if in no other, Thomas deservedly should be seen as the martyr of Trowbridge.

After - we don't know how long after - his interment, a gravestone was erected 'at his earnest request' by the shearmen of Yorkshire, Wiltshire and Somerset to commemorate his memory. The first stone made suitably dutiful noises about contrition: 'He died a true penitent, being very anxious in his last moments that others might take a timely warning and avoid evil company.' But when the old stones fell into disrepair, the cloth workers of the new industry rebuilt the tomb with a panel of their own which reflected what local opinion had all along believed: 'he was afterwards believed to be innocent but determined rather to die than give testimony which would have saved his life but forfeited the lives of others.'

Thomas Helliker's tomb stands there today, a powerful reminder of the very real human cost of resisting 'progress'.

This chapter draws upon the author's Riotous Assemblies: Popular Protest in Hanoverian England by Randall (Oxford University Press, 2006), pp.327-331, by kind permission of Oxford University Press.

The speakers

Prof Adrian Randall is Professor of English Social History and a Pro-Vice Chancellor at the University of Birmingham. He has published numerous papers and books and is widely acknowledged as an expert in the history of popular protest, radicalism, social unrest and labour organization.

Derique Montaut is a Labour Councillor for Swindon Borough Council, a former Group Leader. His interest in left-wing politics began in the 1960s when he left London to work in Swindon where he came an active Trades Union Shop Steward in one of the biggest plants producing pressed steel parts for cars.

Dave Chapple has been a Somerset postman and local historian for 33 years. He is a militant activist in the Communication Workers Union, and Secretary of Bridgwater Trades Union Council. His research interests include Somerset coal-miners, Somerset farm labourers, and 20th Century West Country Labour and Communist Party history. Dave's latest book is a history of Bristol Post Office Workers.

Nigel Costley is the Regional Secretary of South West TUC. He is a well informed campaigner and as the voice of the TUC is one of the most respected and influential speakers in the region on subjects ranging from the regional economy, migrant workers, housing, Europe, the environment, industrial relations and the history of the trades union movement.

Steve Poole is Reader in English Social and Cultural History at the University of the West of England and Director of its Regional History Centre. He has published widely on popular culture and social protest in 18th and 19th century Britain, much of it with a regional focus on South West England

Rosie MacGregor is the Chair of the White Horse (Wiltshire) Trades Union Council, and an active member of UNISON, having been South West Regional Convenor of UNISON for 10 years until 2009, during which time she spoke on a variety of public service issues on numerous platforms including the Trades Union Congress.

Picture by Bob Naylor

From left, Prof Adrian Randall, Rosie MacGregor, Nigel Costley, Derique Montaut, Dave Chapple and Steve Poole.